THE BOOK AND CD-ROM THAT WORK TOGETHER

SENSES

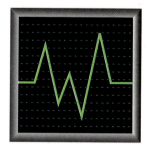

Published in the United States and Canada by
World Book, Inc.
233 N. Michigan Ave., Chicago, IL 60601

All rights reserved. No part of this publication may be reproduced, stored in a retrieval system, or transmitted in any form or by any means electronic, mechanical, photocopying, recording, or otherwise, without prior written permission of the publisher.

ISBN: 0-7166-7233-2
LC: 98-74918
For information on other World Book products, call 1-800-975-3250,
or visit us at our Web site at http://www.worldbook.com

Created by
act-two
346 Old Street
London
EC1V 9RB

Disk
Creative Director: Jason Page
Programming Director: Paul Steven
Art Director: Sarah Evans
Designer: James Evans
Editor: Lyndall Thomas
Programmer: Colette McFadden
Consultant: Graham Peacock
Illustrators: Michele Egar, Jon Stuart,
James Jarvis, Carlo Tartaglia
Production Director: Lorraine Estelle
Project Manager: Joya Bart-Plange

Book
Creative Director: Jason Page
Editor: Lyndall Thomas
Author: Monica Byles
Designer: Michele Egar
Photography: Paul Bricknell, Toby Maudsley
Consultant: Graham Peacock
Production Director: Lorraine Estelle
Project Manager: Joya Bart-Plange
U.S. Editor: Shawn Brennan, World Book Publishing

2001 printing

Copyright © Two-Can Publishing Ltd., 1999
"act-two" and "Interfact" are trademarks of Two-Can Publishing Ltd.
World Book and the globe logo are registered trademarks of World Book, Inc.
Microsoft and Windows are registered trademarks of Microsoft Corp.
Macintosh is a registered trademark of Apple Computer, Inc.

2 3 4 5 6 7 8 9 10 05 04 03 02 01

Printed in Malaysia by Tien Wah Press

Photographic Credits: Front cover: Tony Stone Images
p.9 (top) ZEFA, p.9 (bottom left) ZEFA, p.11 (top) ZEFA, p.12 (center) ZEFA, p.13 (top left) ZEFA, p.14 (top right) ZEFA,
p.15 (top right) Bruce Coleman, p.17 (top right) ZEFA, p.20 (bottom) Hutchison, p.21 (top) Hutchison,
p.23 Bruce Coleman, p.24 (top right) Bruce Coleman, p.29 (top) Bruce Coleman, p.30 (center left) Hutchison,
p.33 Guide Dogs for the Blind Association
Illustrations by Nancy Anderson

INTERFACT

THE BOOK AND CD-ROM THAT WORK TOGETHER

INTERFACT will have you hooked in minutes — and that's a fact!

🔴 **The disk is full of interactive activities, puzzles, quizzes, and games that are fun to do and packed with interesting facts.**

The nutty professor is here to help you with all your questions about the senses.

🟠 **Open the book and discover more fascinating information highlighted with lots of full-color illustrations and photographs.**

Read all about how your senses help you understand the world around you.

🟡 **To get the most out of INTERFACT, use the book and disk together. Look for the special signs called Disk Links and Bookmarks. To find out more, turn to page 41.**

BOOKMARK

DISK LINK
Take your senses on an adventure when you play **SENSELESS**.

Once you've launched **INTERFACT**, you'll never look back.

LOAD UP!
Go to **page 40** to find out how to load your disk and click into action.

What's on the disk

HELP SCREEN

Learn how to use the disk in no time at all.

These are the controls the Help Screen will tell you how to use:
- arrow keys
- text boxes
- "hot" words

EYE OPENERS

You won't believe your eyes once you have seen these optical illusions!

Learn all about vision as you take a close look at these optical tricks. You can even try creating some illusions of your own. You'll find more than meets the eye!

 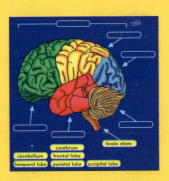

GRAY MATTER

Put some of your brain power to use!

See if you can label the parts of the human brain. Then click on each part to find out more. You'll learn about the control centers for each of the senses.

MAKING SENSE

Ask the experts for the information that you've been looking for!

Meet the nutty professor and his brainy friend! They have the necessary know-how to answer all your questions about the senses.

SENSELESS

Take part in a sensational interactive adventure!

Help! Oliver has been kidnapped and he needs you to help him escape. Use your knowledge of the senses to guide Oliver through the game. Stay alert for the hidden clues along the way.

HEAD TO TOE

Here's your chance to put the senses to the test!

Meet Sensitive Sam and discover how his senses respond to the items on screen. Examine his body with your mouse and put each of his senses to the test.

FACE FACTS

Are you ready to face up to this challenging quiz?

Try this quiz to see if your knowledge of the senses is up to snuff. Can you get enough correct answers to put some sense back into Susan's face?

HEAR, HEAR

Sound off to learn about hearing!

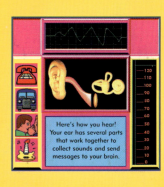

Spend some time at the sound factory and discover how the ear works. Experiment with different sounds to learn all about decibels and frequency.

What's in the book

8 **What are the senses?**
Understanding the world around you

10 **Busy messengers**
The brain and nerves in action

12 **Sight**
Take a closer look at the eye

14 **Dark and bright**
How does light affect the way that you see?

16 **Smell**
Getting to know the nose

18 **Scent and savor**
Sniffing around for different smells

20 **Taste**
Find out how your tongue works

22 **Sweet and sour**
Experiments to tantalize your taste buds

24 **Touch**
Get under your skin to find out about touch

26 **Hot and cold**
How does your body react to temperature?

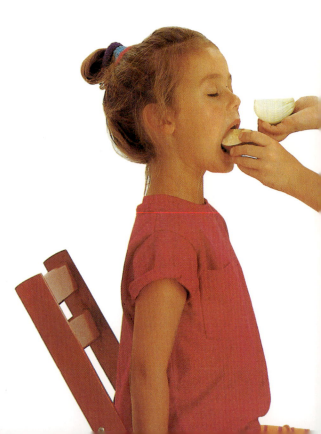

*All words in the text that appear in **bold** can be found in the glossary*

28 **Hearing**
Examine the inner regions of the ear

30 **Loud and soft**
Not all sounds are music to your ears!

32 **Different worlds**
Living without one of the senses

34 **Glossary**
Key words defined

36 **Lab pages**
Note pages for you to photocopy and use

38 **Loading your INTERFACT disk**
How to load your disk

40 **How to use INTERFACT**
Easy-to-follow instructions

42 **Troubleshooting**
Got a problem? Find the solution here!

44 **Index**
The quick route to information

What are the senses?

When you wake up in the morning, do you feel the warmth of your bed, switch off the alarm, look around the room, listen for sounds in the house, and sniff for breakfast?

All of these actions involve your senses. People have five senses that receive messages from the world around them: sight, hearing, smell, touch, and taste. These messages provide us with useful information, such as whether a situation is dangerous, whether food is available, or how close or far away something is.

DISK LINK
What about hunger or thirst? Find out about the internal senses in MAKING SENSE.

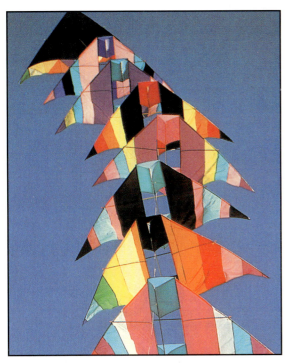

Your senses also give you information about things that are attractive in the environment around you, such as bright colors or beautiful scents. Advertisers often use bright colors to make products attractive to customers. In the natural world, bright colors may have developed for display purposes, or to act as a warning.

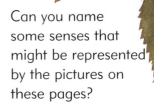

Can you name some senses that might be represented by the pictures on these pages?

Busy messengers

Your eyes, ears, tongue, nose, and skin are working all the time, receiving information from the world around you. Even as you sleep, they send signals to your **brain**.

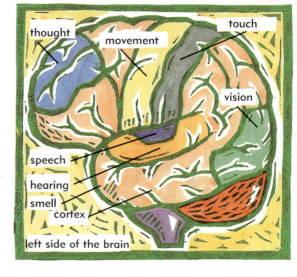

left side of the brain

▲ Your brain is made up of billions of tiny **cells**. The wrinkly outer layer of the brain is called the **cortex**. Messages from your tongue, eyes, ears, nose, and skin pass along **nerves** to special areas of the cortex, each concerned with a particular sense.

▼ As you look at these strawberries, a message travels from your eyes to your brain. The brain sends signals to the rest of your body, and then your mouth starts to water and you begin to feel hungry.

▼ Young puppies cannot see well, so they use their strong sense of smell to nuzzle their way to their mother's milk.

DISK LINK
You can take a closer look at each of the parts of the brain in GRAY MATTER.

▶ Take care before touching hot things. When you touch something hot, your spinal cord receives an alarm message from the nerve endings in your skin. Your spinal cord will quickly tell your **muscles** to pull your hand away if an object is hot enough to hurt you.

Sight

Only a small part of your eye can be seen from the outside of your body. Your eyeball is actually the size of a ping-pong ball, and it is set back into your skull. Your eyelids, eyelashes, and eyebrows keep dirt out of your eyes. Every few seconds, your eyelids blink, covering your eyes with salty tears. Tears help keep your eyeballs moist and remove dirt or dust that gets in.

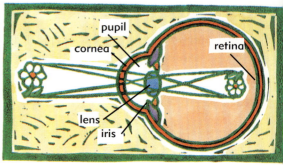

▲ An image is made up of light reflected from an object. As your eyes receive light, it passes through the **cornea** and enters the **pupil**. The light then passes through a **lens**, which turns the image upside down and brings it into **focus** on the light-sensitive cells of the **retina**. These cells send the upside down image to the brain. The brain turns the image right side up.

▲ Your two eyes see things from slightly different angles. The brain combines the two images and judges depth and distance. This makes a three-dimensional picture. Chameleons can swivel their eyes around in their sockets, or even turn one eye forward and the other eye backward. Chameleons can see in two directions at the same time, which helps them to watch out for danger and food.

◀ Hawks use their excellent eyesight to spot prey moving on the ground far below.

◀ A fly's eye is made up of thousands of tiny lenses, each one facing a different direction. The fly's brain sees an image in pieces, rather than as a single picture.

▲ Make some cardboard glasses. Cut one red lens and one green lens from colored cellophane. Draw pictures in red and green and look at them through the glasses. Close one eye, then the other. What happens to the pictures?

◀ Put a variety of objects on a tray. Ask a friend to look at the objects for two minutes, then cover the tray with a cloth. How many things can your friend still remember? Now you try. Who can remember more objects?

Dark and bright

The pupil is the tiny hole in the eye. The colored **iris** changes the size of the pupil. The pupil controls the light that enters the eye. In dim light the pupil gets larger, and in bright light it gets smaller.

▲ Giraffes have good eyesight to watch out for danger over long distances.

▲ Turn off the light and close the curtains in a room. Point a flashlight so that a little light falls near the face of a friend. Look at one of your friend's eyes. How big is the pupil? Shine the flashlight closer to the eye. Does the pupil grow bigger or smaller? Now look at the other eye. Has the pupil of that eye changed size?

▶ Cats can see much better in the dark than people can. At night, their large pupils widen so that the reflective layers at the back of their eyes can receive extra light. In bright sunlight, a cat's pupils close to form narrow slits.

DISK LINK
Try playing some more tricks on your eyes in EYE OPENERS.

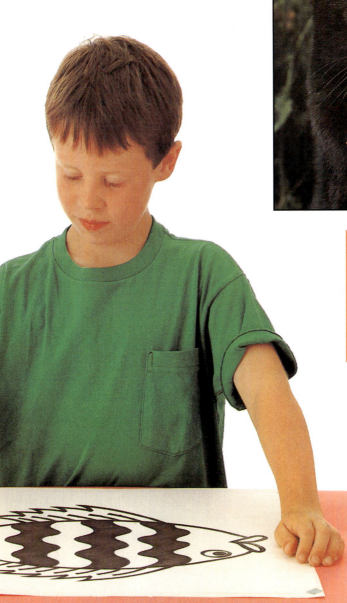

◀ Draw or paint a shape with thick black lines on plain white paper. Stare at it for at least one minute. Now close your eyes tightly. What do you see? For a short while, your brain will keep producing a reverse of the image, white on black, similar to a photographic negative.

15

Smell

You use your nose to breathe air in and out. Your nose is very sensitive and can detect many different smells from the air that you inhale, or breathe in.

▼ How well can you smell? Blindfold a friend and ask her to identify different foods and flowers by sniffing them. You could try orange juice, ginger, mustard, and lavender. Can she tell them apart? Now, mix two of them together.

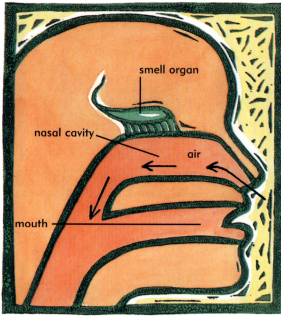

▲ When you inhale, air is drawn into your nose. It passes over the tiny hairs that line the nasal cavity to trap dirt or dust. When the air reaches the back of the nose, it passes over a nerve-packed **membrane**. The nerves send signals to the brain, and these signals are interpreted as smells.

DISK LINK
How does Sensitive Sam's nose react to nice smells and bad ones? Find out in HEAD TO TOE.

Can your friend still tell which is which? Who is the best sniffer in your group of friends? Other things you could include in the smell test are slices of cucumber, lemon, roses, cheese, carrots, garlic, or peppermint.

▲ These arctic wolves have long, large noses. Dogs' noses are 1 million times more sensitive than a person's nose, so they can detect smells that most people would not notice. A powerful sense of smell helps wild dogs find food and distinguish between friends and enemies.

Scent and savor

Some people, such as wine tasters, use their sense of smell at work. Perfume makers can tell up to 10,000 different smells apart. But with a cold, even they would find it hard to smell because the nose becomes blocked with **mucus**.

DISK LINK
Get a whiff of this! These pages contain clues that will help you when you play SENSELESS.

Pleasant scents are often added to perfume, bath oil, foods, and stationery to make them more appealing. Some scents are made artificially, but many are made from natural sources, such as flower petals. Other scents are used to repel. For example, moths keep well away from fabrics stored with moth balls.

▲ Have you ever noticed how bad food smells when it begins to spoil? This is nature's way of warning you not to eat food that could make you ill. **Bacteria** start to grow on old food and break it down, releasing the bad odor. You may see signs of mold, too.

◀ Make a scratch-and-sniff card. Draw a shape on a piece of cardboard and then glue different kinds of herbs or spices onto different areas of the drawing. It should look quite colorful. Can your friends tell which substances you used by sniffing the card? You could use the card for a special friend's birthday.

19

Taste

Your tongue has two important jobs to do. It helps you to shape words so that you can talk. But it also allows you to taste and eat food. It sorts and shapes food as you chew and swallow.

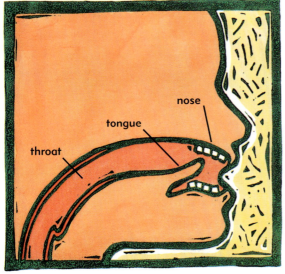

▶ Do you like eating seafood, such as mussels? Across the world, people enjoy eating a huge variety of foods. Aborigines in Australia love fat, white wichety grubs, which they eat fresh or roasted over a fire. Other unusual delicacies people eat include chocolate-covered insects, such as locusts and grasshoppers; dried seaweed; frog's legs; snails; and snakes. Which food tastes best to you?

▼ These sticks of edible clay are eaten by some Nigerians. The clay is a valuable source of calcium in their diet. Calcium is a **mineral** that the body uses to make the teeth and bones strong. Everyone needs to eat a balanced mixture of minerals, vitamins, fats, fiber, and carbohydrates to stay healthy.

▲ When you chew and swallow food, your mouth produces a liquid called **saliva**. It is released by the **glands** in your tongue and cheeks and mixes with the food in your mouth to make a smooth, wet paste. Saliva also starts to **digest**, or break down, the food.

▼ Smells affect your sense of taste. Ask a friend to shut her eyes and then hold an onion to her nose. Let her bite into a piece of apple. She will think that she is eating an onion because that is what she can smell.

DISK LINK
Read these pages carefully! They will help you out when you FACE FACTS.

Sweet and sour

When you eat or drink, your sense of taste and your sense of smell are working at the same time to distinguish between the different flavors.

▼ The color of food may make it more or less appealing to you. Put drops of different food colorings into glasses of fruit juice. Can your friends identify each flavor, or are they turned off by the color?

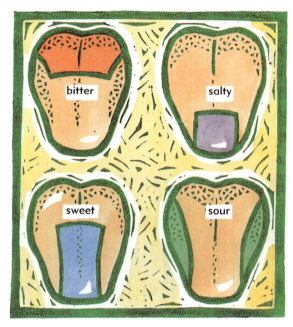

▲ Your tongue is covered with about 3,000 taste buds. Taste buds are tiny hollows in the tongue's surface that are lined with taste-sensitive cells. There are four main types of taste: sweet, bitter, salty, and sour. Some groups of buds are better than others at sensing each type of taste. The buds send messages along the nerves to the taste center in the brain.

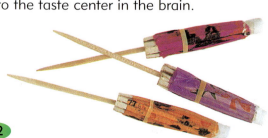

▶ A toad extends its tongue to lick up an earwig. Its tongue can flick out and back again in one-tenth of a second.

▲ A hummingbird has a very long, thin tongue and beak to reach the sugary nectar inside a flower. The nectar contains lots of sugar and tastes very sweet. This provides hummingbirds with the energy that they need to keep their hearts and wings beating rapidly.

Touch

Hot, cold, wet, dry, soft, or prickly: the nerve endings in your skin are constantly giving your brain information about the conditions of your body and the world around you.

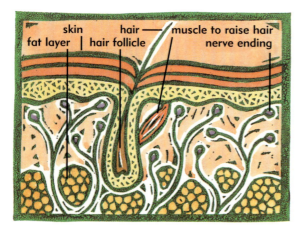

skin | hair | muscle to raise hair
fat layer | hair follicle | nerve ending

▲ A fly triggers touch-sensitive hairs on a Venus's-flytrap. The leaves close to trap the fly, ready for the plant to digest.

▲ Skin is a thin layer covering your whole body. Just beneath the surface of your skin there are nerve endings that send messages to your brain about touch, temperature, and pain. When you are hot, your skin produces **sweat** to cool you down. And when you are cold, the tiny hairs on your skin rise to trap a layer of warm air around you. Every day, millions of cells are lost from the surface of your skin. Your body is constantly making new cells to replace them. Your skin is stretchy, and it moves and grows with your body.

▲ Tickle a friend with a feather. Which areas of skin are the most sensitive?

▼ All people in the world have a unique pattern of tiny ridges on their fingertips, called a fingerprint. The police use fingerprint records to help track down suspects. Keep a file of the fingerprints of your family and friends. Press each finger tip on a stamp pad, then onto paper. Label each set of prints so that you know who they belong to.

▲ The color of your skin depends on how much **melanin** it contains. People with white skin have very little melanin. After a few days in the sun, their skin produces more melanin and develops a tan. People with darker skin have a lot of melanin.

Hot and cold

The nerve endings that tell your brain about touch, temperature, or pain are in groups beneath the surface of your skin. Some areas of your skin are packed with one type of nerve ending, so they are more sensitive to that type of feeling.

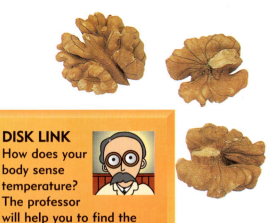

DISK LINK
How does your body sense temperature? The professor will help you to find the answer in MAKING SENSE.

▲ Do you dip your toes into the bath to test the temperature before you get in? The nerve endings in your toes are very sensitive to hot and cold.

◀ Try to identify objects by touch. Make a hole in a box and put some objects with different textures inside, such as a sponge or fruit-flavored gelatin. Ask your friends to put their hands into the box. Can they name each object?

▲ See how cold things affect your sense of touch. Put your fingers in a bowl of melting ice cubes for about 30 seconds. Now touch something very soft and then something prickly. What do you feel? The cold of the ice cubes numbs your nerve endings so they do not send accurate signals to your brain.

Do not touch ice straight from the freezer because it could hurt your skin.

Hearing

Listen to the sounds around you. What is the loudest sound? And what is the quietest? Rub your fingers together near your ear. Is this sound loud or quiet?

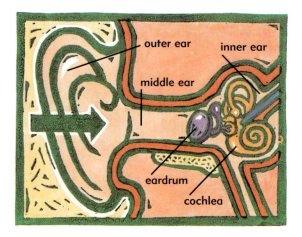

▲ Your ears pick up sounds from the **sound waves** that travel through the air. The outer ear receives the sound waves and directs them into the middle ear. There, the sound waves cause the thin membrane of the eardrum to **vibrate**. Tiny bones in the middle ear also vibrate, causing movements in the liquid inside the **cochlea**. Nerves there change the movements into signals and send them to the brain. The liquid in the cochlea also helps your body to balance.

▼ Place uncooked rice grains or candies on a drum skin. Hold a baking pan above the drum and strike it. Sound waves will travel through the air, causing the drum skin to vibrate, which shakes the rice.

◀ Sounds can travel through solid objects, such as walls or the ground. You might be able to hear an approaching train or truck by putting your ear to the ground.

▶ Dolphins communicate by sending **high-frequency** sounds through the water. They judge distance by the echoes that return. Dolphins can see, hear, and touch but cannot smell.

▲ To avoid bumping into each other by accident, moles tap their heads against the sides of their tunnels. This sends vibrations through the earth and warns other moles to stay away.

◀ Make a telephone! Find two yogurt containers and ask an adult to poke a hole in the end of each one. Push string through the holes and knot the ends so it does not slip through. Get a friend to hold one container and then walk away, pulling the string tight. Ask her to put her container to her ear as you speak into yours. Your voice sends sound waves along the string.

Loud and soft

Many sounds are pleasant, but some can cause harm. At a party or rock concert, the noise may be so loud that you can later hear ringing in your ears. If so, your ears have suffered temporary damage.

▲ Large machinery used in industry, such as mining, or smaller equipment, such as some tractors or jackhammers, can produce deafening sound levels. Workers must wear heavy earphones to protect their ears. Many countries have laws that limit sound levels. Too much noise in the environment is called noise pollution.

▶ Not everyone enjoys listening to the same sounds. Your friend's favorite music may sound terrible to you! Some sounds are too high for people to hear, such as the sounds from dog whistles and some bird, insect, and bat noises. Instead of hearing very low sounds, we feel them as rumbling vibrations.

▲ Next time you hear a vehicle with a wailing siren, listen closely to the sound it makes. The sound will change as the vehicle approaches and passes by. You'll hear the same effect if you ask a friend to blow on a whistle while riding past you on a bicycle. It is not the sound itself that changes, but the way that your ears receive the sound waves.

DISK LINK
How loud is too loud? Test a range of sounds in HEAR, HEAR.

Different worlds

Some people are born without the use of one or more senses, or their senses have been affected by an accident or illness. Often, their other senses become sharper.

▲ Many people wear contact lenses or glasses. The extra lens changes the focus of their eyes. Nearsighted eyes cannot focus on distant objects. Farsighted eyes cannot focus on objects that are close.

THE BRAILLE SYSTEM

CELL

A   B   C   D   E
F   G   H   I   J
K   L   M   N   O
P   Q   R   S   T
U   V   X   Y   Z

▲ In 1829, a Frenchman named Louis Braille created a system of reading and writing for the blind. **Braille** is a series of raised dots, read with the fingertips.

▶ As people grow older, their sense organs become less sensitive. They may need to wear glasses or a hearing aid.

▲ Guide dogs act as eyes for their blind owners. They can signal danger, or tell their owner when to cross a busy road.

▼ People who are deaf can use language systems other than talking, such as signing with the hands and lip reading.

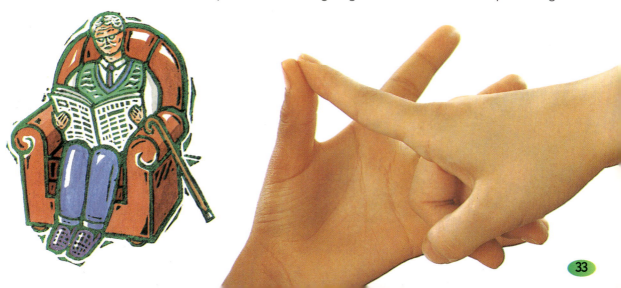

Glossary

Bacteria are tiny life forms. They can live almost anywhere – in the air, water, or soil, on plants or animals, and on food or objects. Some types of bacteria are useful, but others cause diseases.

Braille is a written language used by blind people. It is made up of a series of raised dots that stand for letters and are read with the fingertips.

Brain is the control center of the body. It receives information from the body's senses, stores memories, makes decisions, and organizes the actions of the muscles.

Cell is the smallest part of living matter. All living things are made up of cells.

Cochlea is a tube in the ear. It is filled with liquid and is lined with tiny hairs. Sound vibrations move the liquid, which touches the hairs. Each hair is attached to a nerve that sends a sound signal to the brain.

Cornea is a thin, clear layer that covers the front of the eyeball and the iris.

Cortex is the wrinkled layer of nerves covering the largest part of the brain.

Digest is to break down food and release its energy.

Focus is to make light rays meet, forming a clear image.

Frequency is the number of vibrations per second in a sound wave.

Glands produce chemical substances or help to remove waste products from the body. For example, there are sweat glands in the skin and tear glands near the eye.

Iris is the colored part of the eye. It absorbs strong light and changes the size of the pupil.

Lens is the part of the eye that focuses light on the retina. It is behind the iris.

Melanin is a pigment in the skin, hair, and eyes. It helps protect against sunburn.

Membrane is a very thin and delicate piece of body tissue.

Minerals are solid, nonliving materials from the ground. Calcium, iron, and quartz are examples of minerals.

listening to vibrations

Mucus is a slimy substance that is produced to protect the delicate linings of the body. One type of mucus forms in your nose.

Muscles are large groups of cells that help the body move and function. They are tough and stretchy.

Nerves are long, thin cells that run throughout the body. Some nerves carry messages from the sense organs to the brain. Others process these messages. Still other nerves carry messages from the brain to the muscles, telling them what to do.

Pupil is the small, round hole in the front of the eye.

Retina is the area of light-sensitive cells at the back of the eye. It sends sight signals to the brain.

Saliva is the liquid produced in the glands of the cheeks and tongue. It moistens food, making chewing and swallowing easier. Saliva also starts to digest food.

Sound waves are the vibrations that carry sound through the air, through water, or over solid objects.

Sweat is the salty liquid that is created by the skin to cool the body.

Vibrate is to move rapidly back and forth. Sound travels as vibrations.

Lab pages

Photocopy these sheets and use them to make your own notes.

Running your INTERFACT disk

Your INTERFACT CD-ROM will run on both PCs with Windows and on Apple Macs. To make sure that your computer meets the system requirements, check the list below.

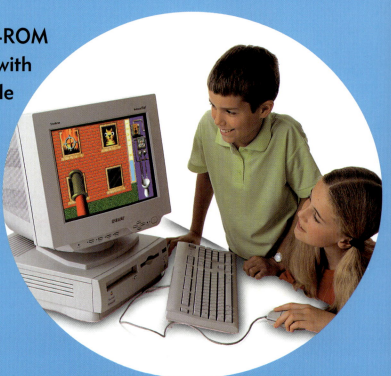

MINIMUM SYSTEM REQUIREMENTS

PC
- Pentium 100 Mhz processor
- Windows 95, 98 (or later)
- 16 Mb RAM
- VGA 256-color monitor
- SoundBlaster-compatible soundcard
- 1 Mb Graphics card
- Double-speed CD-ROM drive

APPLE MACINTOSH
- 68020 processor minimum (PowerMac or G3/iMac recommended)
- System 7.0 (or later)
- 16 Mb RAM
- Color monitor set to at least 640 x 480 pixels and 256 colors
- Double-speed CD-ROM drive

Loading your INTERFACT disk

INTERFACT is easy to load. You can run INTERFACT from the CD-ROM — you don't need to install it on your hard drive. But, before you begin, quickly run through the checklist below to ensure that your computer is ready to run the program.

PC WITH WINDOWS 95 OR 98

The program should start automatically when you put the disk in the CD-ROM drive. If it does not, follow these instructions.

1. Put the disk in the CD-ROM drive
2. Double-click MY COMPUTER
3. Double-click CD-ROM drive icon
4. Double-click on the SENSES icon

CHECKLIST

- Make sure that your computer and monitor meet the system requirements on page 38.
- Ensure that your computer, monitor, and CD-ROM drive are all switched on and working normally.
- It is important that you do not have any other applications, such as word processors, running. Before starting INTERFACT, quit all other applications.
- Make sure that any screen savers for your computer have been switched off.

APPLE MACINTOSH

1. Put the disk in the CD-ROM drive
2. Double-click on the INTERFACT icon
3. Double-click on the SENSES icon

How to use INTERFACT

INTERFACT is easy to use. First see page 38 to find out how to load the program. Then read these simple instructions and dive in!

There are seven different features to explore. Use the controls on the right-hand side of the screen to select the one you want to play. You will see that the main area of the screen changes as you click on different features.

For example, this is what your screen will look like when you play HEAD TO TOE, where you can put Sensitive Sam's senses to the test. Once you've selected a feature, click on the main screen to start playing.

Click here to select the feature you want to play.

Use your mouse to explore Sam's body, or put his senses to the test.

Click on the arrow keys to scroll through the different features on the disk or to find your way to the exit.

This is the text box, where instructions and directions appear. See page 4 to find out what's on the disk.

DISK LINKS

When you read the book, you'll come across Disk Links. These show you where to find activities on the disk that relate to the page you are reading. Use the arrow keys to find the icon on screen that matches the one in the Disk Link.

DISK LINK
Should you always believe your eyes? Find out when you play EYE OPENERS.

BOOKMARKS

As you explore the features on the disk, you'll bump into Bookmarks. These show you where to look in the book for more information about the topic on screen. Just turn to the page of the book shown in the Bookmark.

LAB PAGES

On pages 36 – 37, you'll find note pages for you to photocopy. These are for making notes and recording any thoughts or ideas you may have about what you've read.

HOT DISK TIPS

• If you don't know how to use one of the on-screen controls, simply touch it with your cursor. An explanation will pop up in the text box!

• Any words that appear on screen in a different color and underlined are "hot." This means that you can touch them with the cursor for more information.

• Keep a close eye on the cursor. When it changes from an arrow ➔ to a hand, 👉 click your mouse and something will happen.

• In some of the features, your cursor will change into a special tool, such as a magnifying glass 🔍 or a thermometer. 🌡 When this happens, click on that part of the screen to learn more about what's happening there.

Troubleshooting

If you have a problem with your INTERFACT disk, you should find the solution here. If you still cannot solve your problem, call the helpline at 1-888-732-6564.

YOUR COMPUTER SETUP

RESETTING SCREEN RESOLUTION

Resetting screen resolution in Windows 95 or 98:
Click on START at the bottom left of your screen, then click on SETTINGS, then CONTROL PANEL, then double-click on DISPLAY. Click on the SETTINGS tab at the top. Reset the Desktop area (or Display area) to 640 x 480 pixels and choose 256 colors, then click APPLY. You may need to restart your computer after changing display settings.

Resetting screen resolution for Apple Macintosh:
Click on the Apple symbol at the top left of your screen to access APPLE MENU ITEMS. Select CONTROL PANELS, then MONITORS (or MONITORS AND SOUND) then set the resolution to 640 x 480 and choose 256 colors. Screen resolutions can also be reset by clicking on the checkerboard symbol on the Control Strip.

ADJUSTING VIRTUAL MEMORY

Adjusting the Virtual Memory in Windows 95 or 98:
It is not recommended that these settings are adjusted as Windows will automatically configure your system as required.

Adjusting the Virtual Memory on Apple Macintosh:
If you have 16 Mb of RAM or more, SENSES will run faster. If you do not have this amount of RAM free, hard disk memory can be used by switching on Virtual Memory. Select the Apple menu, Control Panels, then select Memory. Switch on Virtual Memory. Set the amount of memory you require, then restart your machine.

COMMON PROBLEMS

 Disk will not run
There is not enough memory available. Quit all other applications and programs. If this does not work, increase your machine's RAM by adjusting the Virtual Memory (see left).

 There is no sound (Try each of the following)

1. Ensure that your speakers or headphones are connected to the speaker outlet at the back of your computer. Make sure they are not plugged into the audio socket next to the CD-ROM drive at the front of the computer.

2. Ensure that the volume control is turned up (on your external speakers and by using internal volume control).

3. (PCs only) Your sound card is not SoundBlaster compatible. To make your settings SoundBlaster compatible, see your sound card manual for more information.

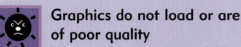 **Graphics do not load or are of poor quality**
Not enough memory is available or you have the wrong display setting. Either quit other applications and programs or make sure that your monitor control is set to 256 colors.

 Graphics freeze or text boxes appear blank (Windows 95 or 98 only)
Graphics card acceleration is too high. Right-click your mouse on MY COMPUTER. Click on PROPERTIES, then PERFORMANCE, then GRAPHICS. Reset the hardware acceleration slider to "None." Click OK. Restart your computer.

 Text does not fit into boxes or hot words do not work (PCs only)
The standard fonts on your computer have been moved or deleted. You will need to reinstall the standard fonts for your computer. PC users require Arial. Please see your computer manual for further information.

 Printouts are not centered on the page or are partly cut off
Make sure that the page layout is set to "Landscape" in the Print dialog box.

 Your machine freezes
There is not enough memory available. Either quit other applications and programs or increase your machine's RAM by adjusting the Virtual Memory (see left).

Index

B
Braille 32
brain 10, 11, 12, 13, 15, 16, 22, 24, 26, 27, 28

C
cell 10, 12, 22
cochlea 28
cold 24, 27
cornea 12
cortex 10

E
ear 10, 28, 29, 30, 31
eye 10, 12, 13, 14, 15, 32

F
focus 12
food 8, 19, 20, 21, 22
frequency 29

G
glands 20

H
hearing 8, 28-29, 30-31
heat 11, 24, 27

I
iris 12, 14

L
lens 12, 13
light 12, 14, 15

M
minerals 20
muscles 11

N
nerves 10, 11, 16, 22, 24, 27, 28
nose 10, 16, 17, 18, 20, 21

P
pupil 12, 14, 15

R
retina 12

S
saliva 20
sight 8, 9, 10, 11, 12-13, 14-15, 32, 33
skin 10, 11, 24, 25, 26, 27
smell 8, 11, 16-17, 18-19, 21, 22, 29
sound 28, 29, 30, 31
sweat 24

T
taste 8, 20-21, 22-23
taste buds 22
tongue 10, 20, 22-23
touch 8, 9, 11, 24-25, 26-27

V
vibration 28, 29, 30

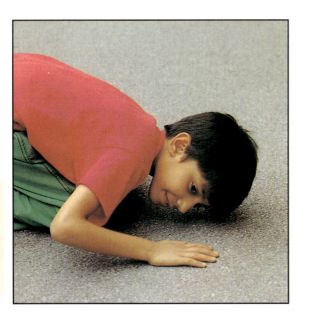

CHECK OUT THE WHOLE INTERFACT SERIES

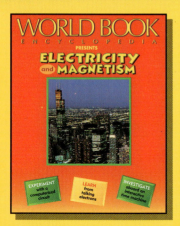

CD (PC/MAC) ISBN 0-7166-7209-X

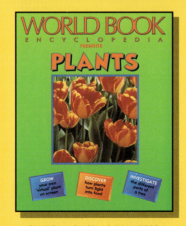

CD (PC/MAC) ISBN 0-7166-7239-1

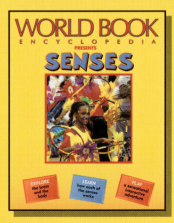

CD (PC/MAC) ISBN 0-7166-7233-2

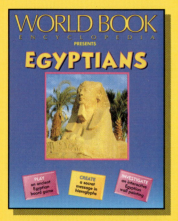

CD (PC/MAC) ISBN 0-7166-7206-5

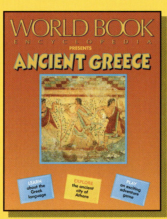

CD (PC/MAC) ISBN 0-7166-7234-0

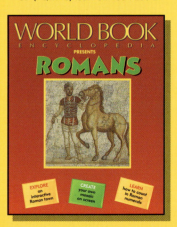

CD (PC/MAC) ISBN 0-7166-7215-4

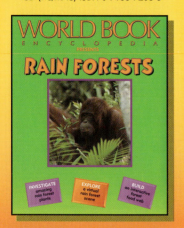

CD (PC/MAC) ISBN 0-7166-7230-8

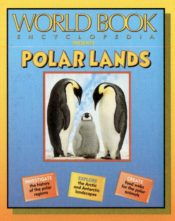

CD (PC/MAC) ISBN 0-7166-7227-8

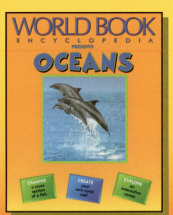

CD (PC/MAC) ISBN 0-7166-7212-X

WATCH FOR NEW TITLES!

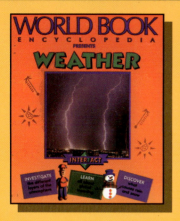

CD (PC/MAC) ISBN 0-7166-7236-7

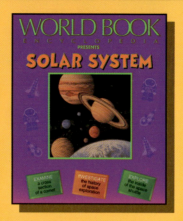

CD (PC/MAC) ISBN 0-7166-7218-9

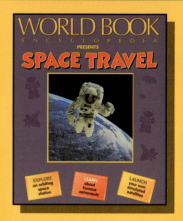

CD (PC/MAC) ISBN 0-7166-7202-2

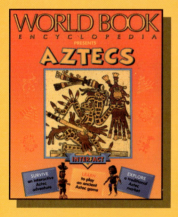

CD (PC/MAC) ISBN 0-7166-7250-2

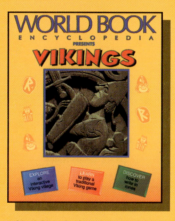

CD (PC/MAC) ISBN 0-7166-7221-9

There is a wide array of **INTERFACT** titles to choose from, covering science, history, and nature.

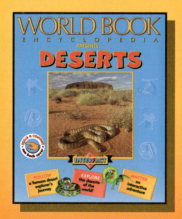

CD (PC/MAC) ISBN 0-7166-7203-0

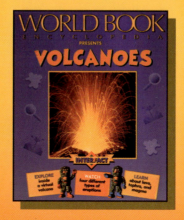

CD (PC/MAC) ISBN 0-7166-7224-3

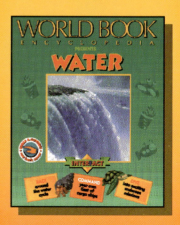

CD (PC/MAC) ISBN 0-7166-7291-X

MORE NEW TITLES

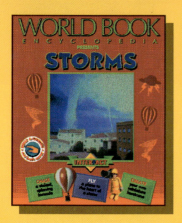

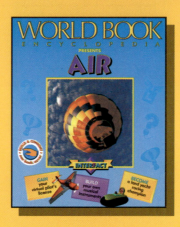

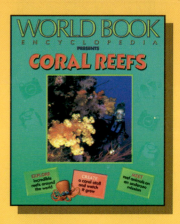

CD (PC/MAC) ISBN 0-7166-7290-1 **CD** (PC/MAC) ISBN 0-7166-7289-8 **CD** (PC/MAC) ISBN 0-7166-7288-X

INTERFACT REFERENCE

Look for the new **INTERFACT REFERENCE** series.
Each large, colorful book works with an exciting disk, opening up
whole new areas of learning and providing a great reference source.

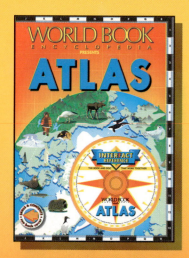

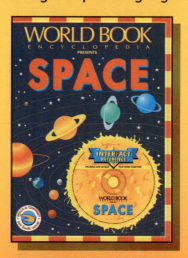

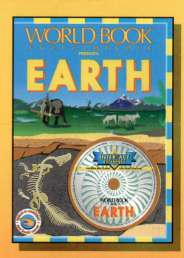

CD (PC/MAC) ISBN 0-7166-9910-9 **CD** (PC/MAC) ISBN 0-7166-9912-5 **CD** (PC/MAC) ISBN 0-7166-9911-7